THE LITTLE BOOK OF

MUSIC THEORY

An essential introduction to the language of music.

D1054100

Amsco Publications
New York/London/Paris/Sydney/Copenhagen/Madrid

CONTENTS

INTRODUCTION

Have you ever wanted to understand more about music, or write your own?

This book will give you an introduction to the language of music and help you understand its essential simplicity. So if you have ever been curious about how music works, this is the book for you. The concepts explained here are common to all Western music, be it classical, pop, rock, folk, blues, or soul. If you've ever wanted to write your own music, an understanding of these fundamental concepts will help.

Once, only writers on classical music talked about music theory. Today it's not unusual to see a discussion of music theoy in a book on popular music. Whether you're a singer or an instrumentalist, a member of a string quartet or a rock band, or just someone who loves listening to music—knowing a little theory will enhance your awareness and increase the pleasure music gives you.

This book is supplemented by *The Little Book of Musical Terms,* a music dictionary containing all the definitions you need for both classical and contemporary music styles.

THE BASICS

Centuries ago, musicians developed a way of preserving music and teaching it to other musicians. This was the beginning of the standard music notation used today.

The Staff

The musical staff consists of five lines. Notes are placed on or between the lines, lower or higher according to their pitch.

Staff

The Treble Clef

The treble clef circles around the second line of the staff. This indicates that a note on this line is a G note. For this reason the treble clef is also sometimes known as the G clef.

Treble Clef

Letter Names

There are seven note letter names in music: A B C D E F G. These correspond with the white notes of the keyboard, where the sequence is repeated several times.

The lines of the treble staff correspond with the notes E G B D F. Here's an easy way to remember this—think of the phrase Every Good Boy Does Fine. The spaces within the staff spell the word FACE. The space immediately below the staff is D and the space above it is G.

E G B D F   F A C E   D G

The Bass Clef

There are other clefs which change the meaning of the staff's lines. After the treble clef, the most common is the bass or F clef. This is used for the left hand of a piano part, and for low-pitched instruments such as bass guitar.

The bass clef features two dots on either side the fourth line of the staff. This indicates that a note on the fourth line is a F note. The lines on the staff now correspond to the notes G B D F A. The spaces spell out A C E G.

G B D F A   A C E G   F B

Leger Lines

Leger lines are used to show higher or lower notes. These lines can be placed above or below the staff.

Several leger lines can be attached to a note, but the more you use, the harder it is for the eye to take them in at a glance. If a piece of music involves a long succession of high leger notes, the symbol *8va* can be placed above the staff and the notes written one octave lower than they sound. As you can see this makes the music easier to read.

Transposing Instruments

Certain instruments are not written at exactly the pitch at which they sound. This is because their range, written at the strict pitch, would take them too much above or below a staff. Such instruments are called transposing instruments. The notes they play actually sound at a different pitch than the same notes played by a non-transposing instrument (such as a piano). Music for these instruments is usually written in a different key. This enables musicians to play the same piece of music together.

Middle C

The note Middle C is commonly used by musicians as a reference point. As there are other C notes we have to be able to distinguish among them. The note Middle C has a frequency of 256Hz. This is the C note nearest to the middle of a piano keyboard.

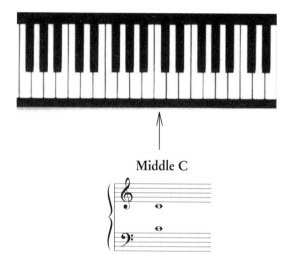

Middle C

Middle C is written on the first leger line below the treble clef—or on the first leger line above the bass clef. This is the same note. The treble and bass clefs are separated in order to make notes easier to read—and to distinguish between the left and right hands on the keyboard.

The music for many instruments can be written on one clef. The piano is an exception because it has a very wide range of notes, from low to high. Consequently, it needs a bass clef (for the left hand) and a treble clef (for the right hand). The two staves are joined by a bracket, as shown.

Guitar Tablature

Another type of notation is popularly used for guitar, music, called guitar tablature.

The six lines represent the actual strings of the guitar. Tablature, or TAB as it is abbreviated, is not a modern invention. A similar form of notation was used in the 16th century for instruments such as the lute.

Fret numbers are written on the lines so that the player sees immediately which fret to play on which string.

The disadvantage of tablature is that it does not give an indication of rhythm, so usually it is combined with a traditional staff to provide a fuller picture of the music.

Here is an example of tablature for the bass guitar:

Unlike the piano, stringed instruments such as the guitar often allow you to play the same note in more than one place. A player can choose where to play the note, and which fingering to use. Tablature makes it clear to the player at what position to play each note.

Here's a handy reference guide to some of the most common notations in TAB.

THE MUSICAL STAFF shows notes and rests and is divided by lines into bars. notes are named after the first seven letters of the alphabet.

THE TABLATURE STAFF graphically represents the guitar fingerboard. Each horizontal line represents a string, and each number represents a fret.

4th string, 2nd fret

1st & 2nd strings open, played together

open D chord

HALF-STEP BEND: Strike the note and bend up one half-step.

WHOLE-STEP BEND: Strike the note and bend up one whole step.

GRACE NOTE BEND: Strike the not and bend as indicated. Play the first not as quickly as possible.

QUARTER-TONE BEND: Strike the note and bend up a quarter step.

HAMMER-ON: Strike the lower note with one finger, then sound the higher note (on the same string) with another finger by fretting it without picking.

PULL-OFF: Place both fingers on th notes to be sounded. Strike the first no and without picking, pull the finger of sound the lower note.

BEND & RELEASE: Strike the note and bend up as indicated, then release back to the original note.

LEGATO SLIDE (GLISS): Strike the first note and then slide the same fret-hand finger up or down to the second note. The second note is not struck.

SHIFT SLIDE (GLISS & RESTRIK Same as legato slide, except the second note is struck.

ACCIDENTALS

Introduction to Intervals

The distance between two pitches is called an interval. The smallest interval used in most Western music is called the half-step. This is the distance between any two keys on a piano keyboard. This means that halfway between A and B is another note. You can think of this as either A plus a half-step (A sharp), or B minus a half-step (B flat).

Sharps, Flats, and Naturals

A sharp sign (♯) raises the pitch of any note by a half-step. A flat sign (♭) lowers the pitch of any note by a half-step. So A♯ and B♭ are the same note and on the piano are played by the same black key. These signs are called accidentals. A *natural* (♮) cancels out the effect of a sharp or a flat. In rare instances a note is sometimes raised or lowered by a whole tone. This can result in a *double sharp* (𝄪) or a *double flat* (♭♭). Thus A𝄪 is actually the same pitch as B.

By introducing the five sharp/flat notes to our original seven we produce this sequence.

A   A♯/B♭   B   C   C♯/D♭   D   D♯/E♭   E   F   F♯/G♭   G   G♯/A♭

Amazingly, all of our music is created using just these twelve notes!

Octaves

We mentioned before that there are several versions of each note on the piano keyboard. For instance, the A note can occur up to eight times on a full-sized piano. These A notes are at different pitches, but sound similar due to their wavelengths and cycles per second. Every twelve half-steps (an octave), the wavelength either doubles (going up the keyboard) or halves (going down).

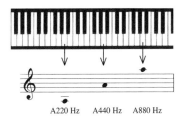

RHYTHM AND TIME

So far we've established how to represent the pitch of a note. But how do we indicate how long it should last, and at what speed to play it?

Note Values

Every note in a composition has a certain length.

Different types of notes are used to indicate specific durations. Here's a quick-reference guide to each note type.

Symbol	Name	Number of Beats
𝅝	whole note	4
𝅗𝅥	half note	2
𝅘𝅥	quarter note	1
𝅘𝅥𝅮	eighth note	$1/2$
𝅘𝅥𝅯	sixteenth note	$1/4$
𝅘𝅥𝅰	thirty-second note	$1/8$
𝅘𝅥𝅱	sixty-fourth note	$1/16$

Here's what the notes look like on the staff. Stems can go up or down depending on various conventions such as which line they are placed on (notes above the middle line tend to have their stems drawn downward) or how many parts are represented at once on a single staff.

Rhythms can be more complicated or subtle than we could write down using just these notes. To represent other rhythms and note lengths, we need a few more types of notes and symbols.

Dotted Notes

A dot placed after a note increases the duration of that note by fifty percent. Here are some examples of dotted notes.

beats: 3 = 2 + 1   1½ = 1 + ½   ¾ = ½ + ¼

Ties

Two notes of the same pitch can be linked together with a tie. Only the first note is played, and the duration of the second one is added on to the first. Dotted notes can also be tied to each other. The tie allows you to create a note value that lasts a fraction longer than a typical note. It also allows you to create a note lasting more than one measure.

Rests

A rest is an indication of silence. This could be for part of a beat, a beat, a whole bar, or many bars at a stretch. Each note type has corresponding rest.

Dotted Rests

A dot placed after a rest adds fifty percent to the original rest value. Here's an example.

1½ beat rest

Beams

Some elements of music notation simply make things easier on the eye. It is difficult to read music that contains many individual eighth notes and sixteenth notes.

Have a look at this example:

It's much easier to see the rhythm patterns when the notes are grouped together with beams.

It is important to remember that musical notation is to some extent approximate. The subtleties of pitch and timing in a singer's voice cannot always be exactly put down on paper. The more precise a system of notation is, the harder it is to read. Standard musical notation is a good compromise between the extremes of simplicity and precision.

Tempo

The speed (tempo) of a piece of music is usually indicated by an Italian term such as *largo, moderato, andante, allegro*—or an English term such as *slowly, moderately,* or *lively.* Sometimes the tempo of a pieces is indicated with a metronome marking.

$$\text{♩}=\textbf{120}$$

This metronome marking indicates 120 quarter-note beats per minute. If you have a metronome or drum machine, you can set it at this speed to indicate this tempo exactly.

Time Signature

Whatever the tempo, and whatever the rhythm patterns found in each bar, almost all music has a constant beat (or *metre*). When you dance to music or tap your foot, you're responding to the beat. The metre of the piece is governed by the time signature, which organizes the overall rhythm of the music.

A time signature is normally found at the beginning of a piece of music. It consists of two numbers.

The top number refers to the number of beats in each measure, and the bottom number indicates which type of note makes up the beat.

Common Time

The most common time-signature is $\frac{4}{4}$, which indicates there are four quarter-note beats in each bar. This time signature may be written in two ways (**C** standing for *common time*):

A measure of $\frac{4}{4}$ can use any number or mixture of notes and rests, provided that the total time value does not exceed four beats per measure.

The following example shows two more patterns of notes that each add up to four beats.

21

The following examples show measures with too many beats. These measures are impossible in $\frac{4}{4}$ time.

Simple Time

Other common time-signatures include $\frac{3}{4}$ (waltz time) and $\frac{2}{4}$ (march time). Some time signatures use a half-note, as the standard beat, such as $\frac{4}{2}$, $\frac{3}{2}$, or $\frac{2}{2}$.

Occasionally you'll find music in $\frac{6}{4}$ time, or even the asymmetrical $\frac{5}{4}$ (as in Dave Brubeck's popular jazz classic "Take Five").

All of these are known as simple time signatures because each beat can be subdivided into two beats of equal value.

Compound Time

Compound time signatures are based on dotted notes—and each beat may be divided into three beats of equal value.

§ is a typical compound time signature. This metre features six eighth-notes in each measure. These are grouped into two pairs of three, which create two emphasized beats per measure. Compare § with ⅜ which has emphasized beats per measure.

Here's an example § time. The first bar shows the characteristic two groups of three eighth-notes.

The first bar of this example in ⅜ time shows how beams are used to indicate three groups of two, instead of two groups of three as in § time.

⅛ time features twelve eighth-notes grouped into four groups of three. § has three stressed beats, each of which divide into three. Compound time signatures such as these have a distinctive bouncy rhythm. Many blues songs are written in ⅛ time.

Unusual Time Signatures

Some less common time-signatures include $\frac{5}{8}$, $\frac{7}{8}$, and $\frac{11}{8}$. These can be disconcerting because they tend to sound like $\frac{6}{8}$, $\frac{4}{4}$, and $\frac{12}{8}$ with one eighth-note missing. The rhythmic consequence of this foreshortening is that the beginning of the next bar always comes half a beat earlier than you except it—a factor which keeps audiences and performers on their toes.

Triplets

It is also possible to split a beat in simple time into three. This is called a triplet. Half notes, quarter notes, eighth notes, and sixteenth notes can all be turned into triplets in this way. The triplet allows for a temporary change of metre which doesn't continue long enough to require a new time signature.

MAJOR KEYS

Almost every piece of music is based on some type of scale.
A scale is a sequence of notes relating to a key, with a fixed pattern
of gaps between each note.

The most important scale in Western music is the major scale, which
comprises seven notes, or "steps."

The C major scale can be played entirely on the white notes of the
keyboard.

You can use this pattern of whole steps and half steps to create any major scale. To create the G major scale, you need to raise the F to F♯.

G Major Scale

whole step whole step half step whole step whole step whole step half step
1   1   ½   1   1   1   ½

When a musician plays in the key of G major most F notes are played as F♯.

Now let's try starting a major scale on F.

To preserve the pattern of whole steps and half steps, you'll need to lower the B note to B♭

F Major Scale

whole step whole step half step whole step whole step whole step half step
1   1   ½   1   1   1   ½

When a musician plays in the key of F major most B notes are played as B♭. This raises the question: Why not use a sharp instead?

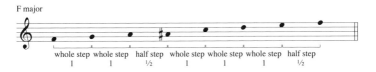

F major

| whole step | whole step | half step | whole step | whole step | whole step | half step |
| 1 | 1 | ½ | 1 | 1 | 1 | ½ |

We could do this, but conventionally, every letter name must be present in a scale. Here there are two A notes. To avoid this confusion, B♭ is used instead of A♯.

The Sharp Major Keys

It is possible to build a major scale from any of the twelve notes. With the exception of C major, which has no sharps or flats, major scales use either sharps or flats—they never mix them. Here are the major scales of the keys that use sharps, in sequence.

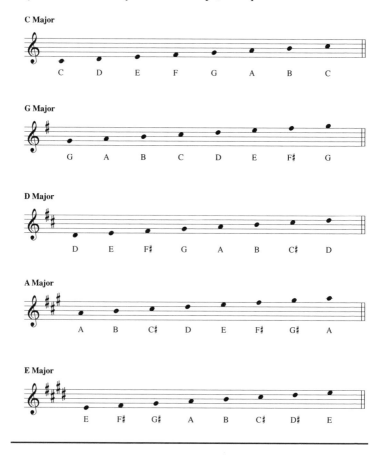

Here are a few tips to help you remember the progression of the major keys that use sharps.

- The new additional sharp always appears on the seventh note of the scale.

- All the sharps in a scale are carried over and automatically become part of the next until all the notes have sharps.

- The starting notes proceed by the interval of a fifth: C G D A E B F♯ C♯.

The key signature always appears at the start of a piece of music and tells you which sharps or flats to play throughout the piece (unless there are accidentals or key changes). The music would look very messy if the four sharps needed for E major were printed in every bar.

The Flat Major Keys

Here are the scales of the major keys that use flats, in sequence.

C♭ **Major**

C♭ D♭ E♭ F♭ G♭ A♭ B♭ C♭

Here are some tips to help you remember the progression of major keys that use flats.

- The new additional flat always appears on the fourth note of the scale.

- All the flats in a scale are carried over and automatically become part of the next until all the notes have flats.

- The starting notes advance by an interval of a fourth: C F B♭ E♭ A♭ D♭ G♭ C♭.

Here's an interesting question: If there are only twelve notes how can there be fifteen major scales?

The answer is that three scales are actually the same, but have different names: D♭ = C♯, G♭ = F♯, and C♭ = B. The reason for this is to simplify the notation and reading of a piece of music. In different settings, one key may be easier to read than another.

A piece of music can begin in one key, change to other keys, and perhaps finish in the original key. Changing key is called *modulation*. To avoid monotony and create the sense of a musical journey, composers frequently change key during longer pieces.

MINOR KEYS

In contrast to major scales, minor scales have a sad quality. While there is only one type of major scale, there are three forms of minor scale: *harmonic, melodic,* and *natural.*

The Harmonic Minor

Take a look at the pattern of whole steps and half steps in the A harmonic minor scale.

A Harmonic Minor Scale

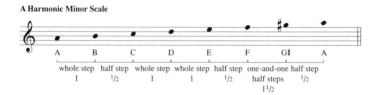

A	B	C	D	E	F	G♯	A
whole step	half step	whole step	whole step	half step	one-and-one half step		half step
1	1/2	1	1	1/2	half steps 1 1/2		1/2

The harmonic minor scale has an angular sound. It is found more in classical music than in popular music. Rock guitarists sometimes use it when they want to produce an exotic, non-Western sound by playing the last four notes of the scale and adding bends to them.

The Melodic Minor

The harmonic minor is not an easy scale for singers. The melodic minor is a variation that is easier to vocalize. Here's the A melodic minor scale.

This scale uses different notes when descending. Ascending, the sixth note is also sharped, thus removing the large gap between 6 and 7 found in the harmonic minor. Descending, the notes are restored to their natural form.

The Natural Minor

Now take a look at the A natural minor scale.

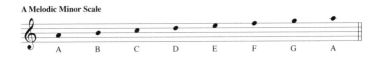

This scale is found in folk music, classical music, and many types of popular music. It is also known as the Aeolian mode.

The Sharp Minor Keys

Each major key has a relative minor which essentially shares the same key signature. The root note of this relative minor is always a minor third (1½ steps) below the major key root note. If you are using the natural minor scale, no additional accidentals will be necessary, unless desired. If the harmonic minor scale is used, one additional accidental will appear in the music which would not be present in the major key. Here are the harmonic minor scales of the keys that use sharps, in sequence.

The Flat Minor Keys

Here are the harmonic minor scales of the minor keys that use flats, in sequence.

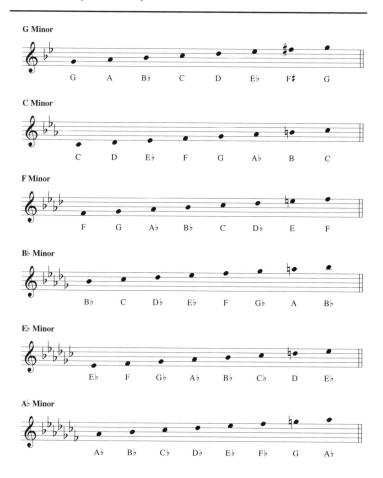

Although these are flat keys, D minor and G minor use sharps for the seventh note, so that every note name is represented.

INTERVALS

As we mentioned earlier, an interval is simply the distance between two notes. This chart features intervals of an octave or less.

Name of Interval	Distance Between Notes (in steps)	Degree of Scale (in C Major)
unison	0	C - C *
minor 2nd	½	C - D$\flat$
major 2nd	1	C - D
minor 3rd	1½	C - E$\flat$
major 3rd	2	C - E
perfect 4th	2½	C - F
augmented 4th	3	C - F$\sharp$
diminished 5th	3	C - G$\flat$
perfect 5th	3½	C - G
augmented 5th	4	C - G$\sharp$
minor 6th	4	C - A$\flat$
major 6th	4½	C - A
minor 7th	5	C - B$\flat$
major 7th	5½	C - B
perfect octave	6	C - C **

* only possible on stringed instruments, where the same note can be played in two different places.

** the distance between one note and the same note an octave higher.

If an interval is greater than an octave, it can be described as a ninth, tenth, eleventh, and so on. These are known as *compound* intervals. The term *diatonic* refers to any interval occurring within the major scale.

Note that when intervals are turned upside-down they reflect other intervals.

minor 2nd	=	major 7th
major 2nd	=	minor 7th
minor 3rd	=	major 6th
major 3rd	=	minor 6th
perfect 4th	=	perfect 5th
augmented 4th	=	diminished 5th

Certain intervals are more commonly used than others. In rock music, the perfect fifth is frequently used in rhythm guitar parts to play power-chords. Heavy rock riffs often use perfect fifths and fourths singly or in combination. Jazz guitarists like using octaves to thicken single-note melody lines. Thirds and sixths are the intervals most commonly used in vocal harmonies.

Here are basic intervals built on C.

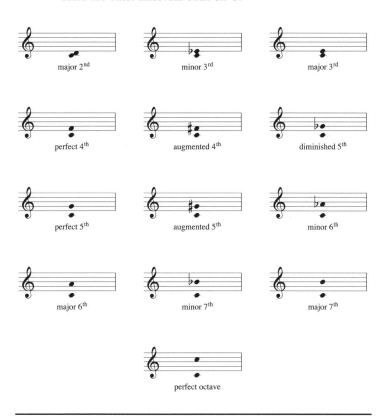

MODES

So far we have looked at the major scale, as well as the natural, harmonic, and melodic minor scales. The major scale and the natural minor were both known to medieval musicians. They called the major scale the Ionian mode and the natural minor scale the Aeolian mode. There were five other modes, which are occasionally used in popular music today.

The Dorian Mode

The Dorian mode is the pattern of intervals found in the sequence from D to D on the white notes of the keyboard.

If this is compared with D natural minor,

you can see that the sixth note is different. Thus the Dorian mode can be thought of as the natural minor with a sharped sixth.

The Dorian scale sounds edgier than the natural minor and is favored by bands like Santana.

The Phrygian Mode

The Phrygian mode is the pattern of intervals found in the sequence from E to E on the white notes of the keyboard.

E phrygian

E   F   G   A   B   C   D   E

If this is compared with E natural minor,

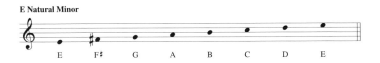

E Natural Minor

E   F♯   G   A   B   C   D   E

you can see that the second note is different. So the Phrygian mode can be thought of as the natural minor with a flatted second. This mode has a distinctly Spanish flavor.

The Lydian Mode

The Lydian mode is the pattern of intervals found in the sequence from F to F on the white notes of the keyboard.

Lydian

F   G   A   B   C   D   E   F

If this is compared with F major,

you can see that the fourth note is different. So the Lydian mode can be thought of as the major with a sharped fourth.

The Mixolydian Mode

The Mixolydian mode is the pattern of intervals found in the sequence from G to G on the white notes of the keyboard.

If this is compared with G major,

you can see that the seventh note is different. So the Mixolydian mode can be thought of as the major scale with a flatted seventh.

Since much of pop and rock music is blues-influenced and features a flat seventh, the Mixolydian is the most common of the five modes.

The Locrian Mode

The Locrian mode is the pattern of intervals found in the sequence from B to B on the white notes of the keyboard.

If this is compared with B natural minor, you can see that the second and fifth are different.

So the Locrian mode can be thought of as the natural minor with a flatted second and fifth. This means that the Locrian scale is the furthest from the normal major or minor scale, and is therefore quite uncommon.

Transposing Modes

Any mode can be transposed to another key. It is possible to have a C Dorian, C Phrygian, C Lydian, C Mixolydian or C Locrian scale. Here's an example of the C Dorian scale.

There are many other types of scales used in different cultures around the world. Here's a quick look at some scales used commonly in rock, pop, and blues.

Pentatonic Scale

There are two main types of pentatonic scale. The major pentatonic scale is merely an edited form of the major scale using scale degrees 1, 2, 3, 5, and 6.

Here's the G pentatonic scale.

Minor Pentatonic Scale

The minor pentatonic scale is an edited form of the natural minor scale using scale degrees 1, 3, 4, 5, and 7.

There are many other minor pentatonic scales possible. This one replaces the seventh with a sixth.

Blues Scale

The blues scale is a minor pentatonic scale with an added sharped fourth. Check out the sound of this one (some blues players never use anything else).

CHORDS

Music consists of melody, rhythm, and harmony—and harmony depends on chords. In this section, we'll take a look at how a chord is formed.

Triads

A chord involves three different notes and is also known as a *triad*. Standard triads are made of two types of intervals: major thirds (two whole steps) and minor thirds (one-and-one-half steps).

Here are the four triad types:

Major triad	C	E	G
intervals		2	1½
Minor triad	C	E♭	G
intervals		1½	2
Augmented triad	C	E	G♯
intervals		2	2
Diminished triad	C	E♭	G♭
intervals		1½	1½

C major   C minor   C augmented   C diminished

These triads can be formed on any of the twelve notes of the scale. Note that the intervals of the major chord are reversed in the minor chord. The only difference between the major and minor chords is the note in the middle (the third of the chord).

These four triad types have different tonal qualities. This is one of the reasons why music is able to evoke complex feelings. For example, the minor triad seems sad in comparison to the major. Most songs use a combination of major and minor chords.

The augmented and diminished chords are used in certain musical contexts. A diminished chord is made up of two minor thirds. This makes it closer to the minor rather than the major. The augmented triad is made up of two major thirds, which makes it closer to the major.

Voicings

If we take the notes of the C major triad and write them on the staff you can see that many different combinations are possible. These variations are called "voicings," which modify the overall effect of the chord.

Inversions

The sound of a chord is also affected by which note is lowest. All of the previous voicings use the root note (C) as the lowest note, and are what is known as *root position* chords.

Here are some C major chords in first and second inversions.

If the third of the chord (E) is the lowest note, it's called a *first inversion* chord. If the fifth of a chord (G) is lowest, a *second inversion* chord is formed.

With a simple triad, only the root position, first inversion and second inversion are possible. If the chord has four notes in it, then it would be possible to have a third inversion, and so on. The number of inversions is always one less than the number of notes in a given chord.

Major Key Chords

The chords that belong to a major or minor key are derived from its scale. Here's the C major scale with the notes of the scale numbered.

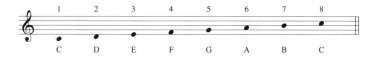

By taking the first, third, and fifth degrees of the scale, we get a C major triad: C E G. If we then do the same thing with D, using the same notes of the scale, we get D F A, the chord of D minor. By doing the same thing on every note of the scale we form the seven primary chords of the key.

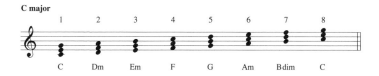

Here are the primary chords in the key of A major.

Here are the primary chords in the key of E♭ major.

We can use a sort of shorthand to talk about each of these seven chords regardless of the key. We can call the chords by the degrees of the scale in Roman numerals: I, II, III, IV, V, VI, and VII. As all major scales have the same internal musical relationships, the sequence of chords always follows the same pattern.

I	II	III	IV	V	VI	VII
major	minor	minor	major	major	minor	diminished

Minor Key Chords

The formation of the chords in a minor key depends on which minor scale is used. Let's take the natural minor scale first.

The Natural Minor

In each case, the primary seven chords follow this pattern.

I	II	III	IV	V	VI	VII
minor	diminished	major	minor	minor	major	major

Here are the primary chords in A the key of minor.

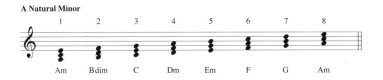

Here are the primary chords in the key of F♯ minor.

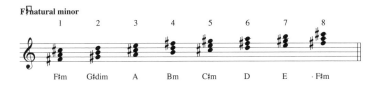

Here are the primary chords in the key of C minor.

The Harmonic Minor

The harmonic minor yields a slightly different result. Here, the primary seven chords follow this pattern.

I	II	III	IV	V	VI	VII
minor	diminished	augmented	minor	major	major	diminished

This pattern is the result of the sharped seventh note of the harmonic minor scale. Here are some examples.

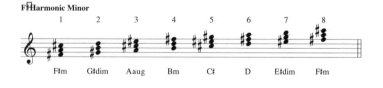

Beyond Major and Minor

So far we have looked at simple major and minor triads. More complex chords can be built by adding notes, or altering the top note (the fifth).

Seventh Chords

You can alter a basic triad by adding the seventh note in the scale to create a seventh chord.

If we did this with the first six chords in the major scale, we would end up with a sequence like this.

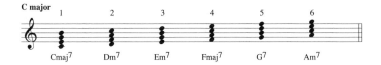

There are three types of seventh chords in this sequence. Let's take a closer look at these chords.

Dominant Seventh Chord

The most common type of seventh chord is the dominant seventh: 1 3 5 ♭7. To form the dominant seventh, simply lower the seventh note of the major scale and add it to the triad. The dominant seventh chord naturally occurs on the fifth note of the major scale. This has a tougher sound than the major seventh.

In blues and blues-influenced music, where flatted notes are introduced into the harmony, the dominant seventh chord is frequently built on chords I, IV, or V.

Major Seventh Chord

The major seventh naturally occurs on the first and fourth notes of the major scale: 1 3 5 7. It has a rich, expressive sound.

Minor Seventh Chord

The minor seventh naturally occurs on the second, third, and sixth notes of the major scale: 1 $\flat$3 5 $\flat$7. It has a melancholy sound, but it is softer than a straight minor chord.

Suspended Chords

Suspended chords (sus4 and sus2) are formed by taking away the third degree of the scale and adding the fourth or second to create a suspension in the harmony. These chords commonly resolve to either a major or minor chord, depending on the key of the piece.

First Octave Chords

Here are the most common types of chords that can be formed by just using a single octave major scale.

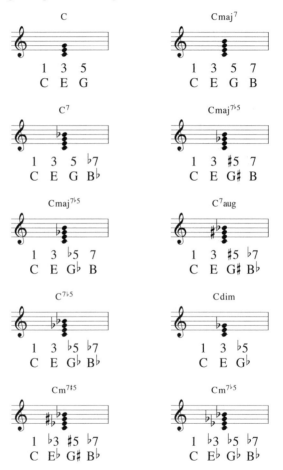

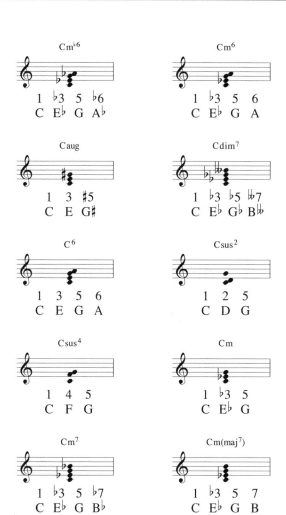

To form more complex chords we can extend the scale to a second octave.

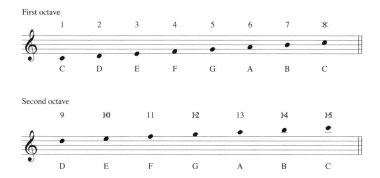

Of these notes, only the 9th, 11th, and 13th are truly meaningful. The 8th, 10th, 12th, and 15th degrees are simply notes of the basic major triad, an octave higher. They don't stand out or alter the sound of the chord in the same way as does the 9th or 11th. The 14th is also irrelevant, as the 7th is used instead.

Second Octave Chords

Here are some examples of second octave chords. All of these may
be played on the piano, but some can only be approximated on the
guitar. A correct thirteenth chord has seven different notes in it—a
guitar has only six strings.

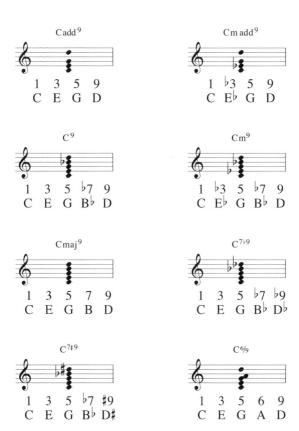

Second Octave Chords (continued)

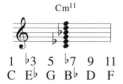

1	b3	5	b7	9	11
C	Eb	G	Bb	D	F

Cm^{11}

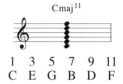

1	3	5	7	9	11
C	E	G	B	D	F

$Cmaj^{11}$

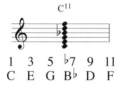

1	3	5	b7	9	11
C	E	G	Bb	D	F

C^{11}

1	3	5	b7	11#
C	E	G	Bb	F#

$C^{7\sharp11}$

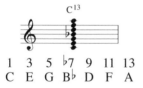

1	3	5	b7	9	11	13
C	E	G	Bb	D	F	A

C^{13}

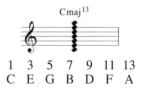

1	3	5	7	9	11	13
C	E	G	B	D	F	A

$Cmaj^{13}$

1	b3	5	b7	9	11	13
C	Eb	G	Bb	D	F	A

Cm^{13}

1	3	5	7	13
C	E	G	Bb	A

$C^{7}add^{13}$

Index